T0290220

How to be Dead in a Year of Snakes

How to be Dead in a Year of Snakes
Chris Tse

AUCKLAND
UNIVERSITY
PRESS

In memory of my Por Por,
Sheut Unn Joe
(1926–2011)

First published 2014
Reprinted 2016

Auckland University Press
University of Auckland
Private Bag 92019
Auckland 1142
New Zealand
www.press.auckland.ac.nz

© Chris Tse, 2014

ISBN 978 1 86940 818 3

A catalogue record for this book is available from the
National Library of New Zealand

This book is copyright. Apart from fair dealing for the purpose of private study,
research, criticism or review, as permitted under the Copyright Act, no part may
be reproduced by any process without prior permission of the publisher.
The moral rights of the author have been asserted.

Cover design: Greg Simpson

Printed by Printlink Ltd, Wellington

I have it in me so much nearer home
To scare myself with my own desert places.
— ROBERT FROST

- *(In which the author interviews a dead man)*

No one asked me to speak, nor took the time to fill a moment with my presence. We cannot hide from ourselves in the dark. I crouch down in the damp void and listen as they pass words about me between themselves like borrowed scandal. The loudest, hungriest voices drown out all reason.

Yes, people talk, talk, talk and say such pointless things. And now, when talking is what will anchor me in their thoughts, such economy of blame will lead us nowhere. They risk my fate of leaving this world nameless.

For years I lit incense and prayed for my share of good fortune, holding fast to the belief that patience brings luck to those who traverse life's terrain with humble expectation. Now such a dispensation numbs me.

I often thought about the things I left behind, how the distance that once indulged me slowly smothered the dreams of those I made promises to. How my wife waited, how my bad luck clung to me like a wandering ghost. We are all losers in a stoic game. Unkind or unsettled, it made no difference in the long run; I took it all like a prize fool.

There is night fading into view with its hoard of loaded pauses, each intake of breath an assertion of my dues. Some stillness makes its way into death's song; some strange madness cocoons me. I suppose having seen their worst at work this may be a good year to fade away.

If I'm to acknowledge *him*, his part in my current state, then I can only say that he might've done it sooner, that if our paths had crossed on any other day or in any other street the outcome would be no different. I'd still be face down in the dirt and for a moment he'd be the bravest man.

And so are we now co-dependent – the scandal that holds the hand of the other? This intimate relationship begs to die a sure death, for there is no comfort in such a connection.

•

1871: first impressions – there is something
unsettling about this country, how its generosity
        of space is inflicted upon bright eyes.

A stone sky meets the cradle
            of New Gold Mountain
        and its promise of good money.

The light spills wild over the landscape.
        Shadows ease into undiscovered terrain.
        Earth shifts   and those first sparks

are short-lived   before a veil of regret
        sickens the view   and needy hands
            scratch at sky for solace.

- *(Good law)*

They made special provisions by virtue to control restricted immigrants (that being the Chinese, and the Chinese alone). *The whole object of the statute was to prevent people of the Chinese race from coming into the Dominion and engaging in industrial pursuits.*[1]

A limitation in number – a fine for not declaring the correct number of Chinese on board – an arbitrary ratio of one Chinaman to every one hundred tons of cargo. *The master of the ship shall be liable to a fine not exceeding one hundred pounds for each such Chinese so carried in excess.* That was our standing in 1905, our lives reduced to administrative shepherding:

- name;
- place of birth;
- apparent age; and
- former place of residence.

They tested our tongues too, to see if we could sound like them, with their words and their ideas of privilege.

No interest in:

- skills;
- past achievements;
- personal ambitions; or
- an openness to change.

Part III [of the Immigration Restriction Act 1908] *is specially devoted to Chinese immigration, which presupposes that the persons at whom it is aimed and who are likely to commit the offences described are ignorant Chinese who know nothing of English or of New Zealand law . . .*[2]

---

1 *Lum v Attorney-General* [1919] NZLR 741 (SC) at 746.
2 *Van Chu Lin v Brabazon* [1916] NZLR 1095 (SC) at 1096.

•

Your wife in Canton –
　　　you carry her in your bones
　　　a private ghost　　　a slippage.

Time is set to thieving
　　　　　your everything
　　　　lost to the barren ink.

She probably moved on
　　　　you tell yourself –
　　a defeated man's consolation –

like so many other left-behind wives
　　　with hearts retreating
　　　　whose husbands broke bones

and endured loaded looks to
　　　provide them with happiness.
　　The echoes of heartache must exist

just as a serpent's trail will taint
　　　the things we neglect
　　　　if we turn from instinct.

•

The accident – your leg crushed
      in the mine – such misery of bone.
     There was menace on the wind that day

riding in to greet one unfortunate soul.
     The fates played their song   its melody
      an echo in your lame limb.

A man can only welcome so much miserable luck,
    courage eventually splintering
      under pressure, so you wished

for death – the easy exit
     from this charade of misfortunes.
      Let death enter

and bring light back into your life
     to stage your great finale. Your fellow
      countrymen would care for your bones

and oversee the finalities –
      perform the proper rituals
      chant the proper words.

The path home   would be free
     from trouble –
      so your heart promised.

•

You picture lanterns blossoming in grey-blue wilderness; the distant lights anchor your gaze. On the surface of your visions you send out boats to the furthest reaches of your desires, pluck the moon from its cradle and hold it in your mouth. This is when you can imagine what would have been if all had gone according to plan, had you become a guest here fully embraced and understood.

Somewhere in the night, layered in the restlessness of the land and the white men's resentment, is the hum of lives spent waiting, withdrawing into their shells. You spend your thoughts drowning in your family – missing from this vista – and contemplate a return with nothing to show for your absence.

When you are stoic the world is cracked, but when you are wishful you see past pain and shadow, soothed by constant light. If you are silent the trees bend away to leave you to your private struggle. If you speak those watchful eyes will study your mettle, trained to tear your thoughts apart.

- *(Eight ghosts)*

The Hanged, *suicides and executions*

The Drowned, *victim possessed in the undertow*

The Depressed and Restless, *seeks redress*

The Headless, *the stray traveller*

The Woman Seeking Revenge, *grace stolen by beasts*

The Kindly Old Woman, *a helping hand*

The Hungry Ghost, *a starving sinner*

The Ghost Who Wanders, *removed and homeless*

• *(SS* Ventnor*)*

kawe mate

The departed   cargo
thought doomed

to forgetful waters

instead finds its way
to open shores

                rescued by the people of the land.

      •••

te rerenga wairua

There is no reason to leave
        the dead   in such a state –

the once-lost must find
their way upon   a bright line.

Death is the common ground
        when acknowledged with respect

gratitude   and the offering of joss.

      •••

karakia

And so the once-lost are salvaged
and laid to rest

among spiritual kin and tender ancestors

to be ghosts who only speak
                    when spoken to

with no choice   in the path they are set upon.

•

What fools we have been
to think we can pack up
our things and leave.

What fools we are
to worship this blue patch,
a mere sky among heavens.

What great distance
is there left?

•

They peer through me as if I were dead.
My hands are tired now, fading to mist.

        •••

I've held out for luck
and fortune like a stony fool,

but sometimes the heart must
gracefully accept defeat.

        •••

These days it feels like I am digging
my own grave.

•

Lionel Terry –

Shepherd of the Nation
Army of One
and
Saint of Order

blind in Winter, thirsty
in the face of blame –

tucks his pleasure into his boots.

• *(Manifesto)*

Come out of The Shadow
with me – your Nature
demands it.

For those who step wild-footed
into communion with the alien
suffer their betrayal.

Strike! That the balance falls upon us
to starve their licentiousness
and we be fools no more.

Strike! That blood shall run to cleanse
great Britain's name, that what we hold dear
is no longer theirs to contaminate.

- *(Charm attack)*

A snake prefers to work alone, calculating his own rhythm. He is a creature of charm, seduction and pursuit, although he will not be pleased with others' excitement – it must be of his design, and his alone.

...

From the beginning Lionel knew he was bound for greatness and thought he might very much like to live forever. To this end he claimed as much space as possible, never looking back.

...

Harmony holds a snake's home intact to reign over voices of the meek.

...

A belly intimate with the earth will not prevent the snake from elevation, through philosophy, deep thought and private schemes.

...

A snake can be slow to forgive and hateful in nature; he is unafraid to settle the score.

...

Lionel was a creature fooled into keeping score for all the wrong reasons. He felt it spreading in his mind, that nameless hollow thrumming with pros and cons. Suspicion.

...

Some snakes tempt with more than just apples.

    •••

They do not know how the snake got in. All they know is that for days they sensed a presence, a tainted breath upon their shoulders.

    •••

That breath found a voice to hook on to.

    •••

However, Lionel wasn't born a snake. Some say he may have been born in a Year of the Dog: loyal, compassionate, *of assistance*.

Still, madness can hide in the most open of minds.

    •••

Indeed, not all men are beholden to the fate with which they are pinned.

    •••

Lionel kept trouble in his blood and it demanded to be soothed.

- *(Disturber)*

Man is proud, but in desperation man will invite a snake
into his home as a good omen. He sees in snakes a will

to survive, how their glossy scales ripple like rumours
and eat the air with their mere presence. A snake adapts.

...

Take pause for constellations; hang prayers to walls.
There is little to feel within a snakeskin home. Build,

destroy, then build again. Stretch and climb, only to fall
again every time we steal the light from one another.

...

When we are old, we will look back upon gold.
When we are time, we will settle for passing.

This is destruction – old forms shift to frame new views
in common-tongue forums. Speak slowly; speak of calm.

...

We can start at the end, where the earth is king, with
a grave and its maggots, with bones stripped of skin.

When the dead are consulted, the world inverts. They are
all restless. It has been so long the sky is now a stranger.

•

On Sunday

the good people go to church,
the roasts are carved

the children play in their gardens, warned
to stay away from *that street*

where they will catch
incurable diseases or disappear

into some Chinaman's shed
never to see daylight again, destined

to become an example
for other children.

On Sunday

Lionel Terry went hunting
for a Chinaman.

•   *(How to be dead in a year of snakes)*

There must always be
a first victim.

Maybe not the very first,
but the one that shocks.

The one that says: *hey, look*.
The one we can't let go.

•

1905: this is the end.   The night opens
to a scene of death –

              gun
              blood
              peanut shells
              a knotted walking stick
              and
              one quiet body.

Two guilty feet
head in an unknown direction

drowned by the pitter-patter
footsteps of those running to help.

Another cold Wellington night
wind on a sharp loop.

Traces of cordite
punctuate the chaos.

His stiff clothes refuse to move
as they lift his body

like a face caught between
photographs – a sick slur
                a busy thought

– just enough to make sense
but still framed with questions.

•

You are silent when they find you –
a tired soul ready to concede,

the no-luck serenade   already soft
                              in your inky sleep.

Face down in your own blood –
blood you should know well

                              a link to every step taken
                              chances gained and lost.

As you bleed out
the night rejects your history –

                              it is only blood
                              after all.

Stir from your edge
and you'll face a new fight.

                              Your bones protest
                              to stay   as is.

This will hurt, more than
your body is willing to accept.

And you will remember nothing
even if you must

                              reach back
                              into madness

and let its unpredictable waves
pull your failing hand under.

So sure this land would cradle you, gift you
gold and riches for your goodness.

                         Instead you lie here
                         removed   returned

waiting for the spirits
to nod.

All this derring-do and still nothing makes sense.
Gather your black luck and hope for the best.

•

Some say it happened so fast –
the piercing bullet and the flesh,
the blood, the fall, the cordite stench.

But for one soul it all plays out
so slowly, as his shapeless form is lifted
in emergency and carried through the unkind night.

The familiar sag of a hospital bed
            beneath
his fallen weight.

The silhouettes of the doctors' hands at work.
Everything fades – their voices
            in fits of panic.

Soon the memory of chance
will leave his body. Hold this moment
            to collect   and accept.

• *(Thoughts of a dying man)*

This constant southern wind laughs through me.
It is cunning   it is deep.

When I turn to catch my shadow
the kūaka pick at my hair   and take hold

lift me like a swollen sack   drag my stubborn weight
towards the mouth of the gust in question.

Gravity does not tether the soul   so I push up
and let the birds take me.   Lonely, lonely

up here in the overture while the footsteps below
dance and smile and make tidy conversation

unbeknownst that the song they hear
is a dead man's tragedy.   Slow sleep.

●

From on high   the light in the valley
begins to stretch   smoothing out

the shadows   that scar the dusk
and the wind appears   to lift last night's

sleep making way for a day of assessment.
Voices of the departed linger.

    ...

From such heights   all exits
are uncovered

          but whose line leads
back to the stains   of this crime?

    ...

From the church   a song of dawn.
The bell rings in another day

though it may as well be for the fallen man
his space   already filling with speculation.

The fantails see the whole of the sky
and fill the clouds   with their opinions.

    ...

Many eyes   see different truths.
They'll want a finger

with which to point
at suspects and victim.

Hold a heart   to each one
and see who triggers   a tell-tale skip.

    ...

Have faith in the certainty
     of guilt.

• *(Chorus)*

Is it right to say the things that are on our minds, to place
ourselves in the eye?   To plot ahead

and slip undetected through the folds of constant babble?
That is the panic of man – a chorus of voices

plummeting in minor keys   towards a vanishing point.
Anyone willing to speak is hindered by their first tongue.

The rain stinks of death.   Where he fell is a battle scar.
Better him than us.

*   *(All together now)*

A merriment of motives
Cause and effect—One foot leads the other—Waiting leads
to disaster.

An ancestry of Chinamen
Gold blood—Crimson skies—White is the colour of death.

A supposition of invaders
A taxing concern—It was the sea—The faster the waves,
the harder the crush.

A counterfeit of alibis
Propaganda—Mass coercion—There is one instance
of truth—Lost and found.

A nourishment of prayers
In a church—The edge of an unknown village—This time
we make do with one tongue.

●

I can see the waver in your eyes –

you've changed the way

you honour   your sky.

●

To kill a man
is to marry a shadow

there   by your side
in the wide-awake night

breathless bedfellow
motionless lover

a heart of silent scorn
mouth stitched shut

a voice unaccounted for
lost among the folds of gossip

he stares at you with eyes
as wide as open graves

●

his name stings the tongue

both of you measured in art

your name now his crime

•

And just like that

      the killer turns himself in.

And just like that

      the shift in the air is a knife

at their throats. The motive

      unstitches their arrangements

and just like that

      history is forged under shadow

by the most conceited voice.

- *(Ghosting—an uncertain fortune)*

The hand carries fortune—a bloom in the fist—having
been seen or seen of—turning back to the outstretched
meanwhile of now—when it is gone do you assume
death or a temporary dislocation?

　　…

Beyond darkest conception—lies a divisive edge
in an exposed world—of a ruse—of a motive
spread—pattern brief, proliferating—scattered
outwash—it is worth noting—how we can be free.

　　…

Motion sustained—the arm as an instrument
of active intent—in search of short-term
satisfaction—here, it fools the weight of its own
conscience—held down—dared to expose its palm.

•

I did not load the gun.

It was the voice of God.

I did not conceal myself in shadows.

It was the night closing in.

I did not wait for a symbolic victim.

It was a stroke of luck.

I did not take aim.

It was a moment of clarity.

I did not shoot.

It was the people's wish.

I did not flee.

It was freedom.

I did not turn myself in.

It was an acknowledgment of service.

I did not start this.

But I will finish it.

•

Every murderer is an artist

       fashioning the ultimate axis of life

is a liar

       shedding many skins

is a thief

       living under gaze of ghosts

is judge and jury

       trialling neither reason nor doubt

is a map

       among the tallest of trees

is a believer

       until the bitter end.

       •••

Every life taken is a bitter lesson

       framed for show

is divine wisdom

       in the pause between breaths

is a return to rightful owners

under watch of night

is day without night and

hours without minutes

is an undiscovered fortune

in a land far from here

is a believer

until the next destination.

- *(In which the author interviews a Mr Terry)*

We must divide the world around us into safety sets or else it splinters of its own accord into anarchy. And if not in our hands then we trust the nation's future to a breed of licentious devils, allowing their sins to wash upon us.

Perhaps we kneel too easily; perhaps the very things that fuel our desires eventually consume us.

First they shake the very ground we walk upon; upset the stable nature of our pioneers.

> (This is before traitors among us
> belittled my actions.)

They shake the sky and demand shelter.

> (Birdsong fills this house; the trapped
> blackbirds herald death.)

They shake their bodies as if swarmed with demons.

> (I've seen rain fall like blood. I've seen sin crawl
> from beneath shadows and into their hearts.)

They may shake my belief in the good of man, but throughout this passage of change I remain,

Lionel Terry.

•

For Death
is no stranger to new starts.

We accept that fire cleanses
as the joss papers burn.

Winds carry the ash to sea and
rid us of this madness of the heart

but occasionally our hands
reach for what once was.

Meanwhile, Murder
(Death's troubled cousin)

never one to learn an honest lesson
takes one heavy step after the other

and makes the same mistakes
at someone else's expense.

•

Put the taste away.

That salt is reserved
for the living
and their fallible
stumbling through life.

Put your sight away.
Illuminate your past
with stolen looks
from thieves and martyrs.

And put your heart away
else it beats helplessly against
the hollow chambers
of your once hopeful days.

If only there remained
some stable core.
Put your breath away. Save it
for the bargaining to come.

Unravel the webs, the lifelines
that ripple from your veins
and sever the tongue that
protests too much.

In this world you've lost
the right to mark their wrongs.
You may have the memory of
death but is it yours to share?

Put your voice away.

• *(Lament for Joe Kum Yung)*

If sunlight had never touched his face
                    would he still hold
            a stoicism of better days
        in the pool of his longings?

He followed tides after listening to those
            who held the sun in their mouths
                words lit upon a curve
        so what was spoken   so what was heard

        – angelic, revelatory –
was kindest to those who listened
                under care of will.
        By the break upon sand   it was all a lie.

If the breath of this land
            was no match to the life that surged
        through his lungs
                back in China –

if his world here were seen through
                a fallacy of glass, vision twisted
        and marred by stolen light –
    only then should you offer to trade places.

So there goes   a life story reduced
        to one gunshot
                and there goes madness
        in the form of public service

and there wait   those graceless thieves
        of light and sound
                slipping to a snake's crawl
                    to rewrite his truths.

• *(Lament for Lionel)*

Surely he will wear
this habit down.
Movement in the earth
keeps him crazed
while private voices
sing the praise of
his violent success.
Like marooned ghosts
they learn to seek out
a cold heart. His steel
is fading. His cause is
the severed head
of an infinite snake.
No – you don't see it
his way, in missions
and hourglasses
shaking faith
to its very foundation.
In fire, the days retreat.
In him, oceans churn.

- *(Following death)*

(every man has his limits   )

(vanishing
       into the crook of night
       like an unspoken thought   )

(scratching elsewhere for light   )

(a bold idea
        now withdrawn
            from usefulness   )

(placed unprotected
                for the welcoming
                duty of death   )

(simmers like a loaded whisper   )

(committed
                to terminating
        where the heavens meet
                the underworld   )

(who's to say such conclusions
            should be dictated
        by the fickle songs of men?   )

●

If time is for the living
do the dead hear clocks ticking?

yes no yes no yes no

Like a live pulse kicking
fresh from concentric containment

swing low swing high

we have prayer
we have ash

we have tea we have flesh

and a wall that casts no shadow.
Anything to keep the omens out.

salt us in the sea

Therein lies darkness and depth
in which to bury the soul

build your cities over our bones

comfort in the meld
pull back the curtain

for the greatest show you'll ever see.

•

We turn
on guesses –

Lionel's sanity questioned
and Joe's history irretrievable.

This settlement hums
and when we clasp our

hands together
the prayers we shake out

are empty.
Deathly, even.

• *(In which the author interviews light)*

I   am   not   petulant;   like   you,
I   am
merely hopeful. Where shadows bleed
must   lie   a   source   of   light.
Light   is   warm   and   sure
of its place in every widescreen vista
or   on   a   stage,   where   it   unfolds
each   scene.   Light   is   proof
that   something   is   happening
right   before   you.
I   am   the   eye.   I   am
the   thought   of   least   resistance.
After   belief
I   make   myself
visible – a golden loose thread.
I   can   be   trusted   –
just watch. This will move them.

                     ...

Here's   where   the   body   fell
–   no,   wait   –
over   *there.*

(There are so many ways to begin
I often confuse myself. Old age
has worn my edges down – nothing
catches,   nothing   drags   me
through   a   life   of   usefulness.
Sometimes   I   can't   decide
where   the   story   truly   starts   or
where   to   place   their   marks.
Each   event   that   punctuates

the arc carries its own intention,
as   does   each   storyteller's
tongue laced with favour and prejudice.
Mine is to seek out the tension and
violence in   their   vibrating hearts.)

Let   me   start   over.
1905:   this   is   the   end.
We   meet   again   –   same   street,
same   sky.
At   first   blush,   the   man   falls
and   stays   down,
language and music fleeing his body,
freed   from   the   limits
of   flesh   and   bone.   From   here,
the   world   extends   into   white
and the voices of the living carry
nothing   but   death.

                    ...

If   I   could   speak
all   you'd   hear   is   echo
over   here
–   no,   over   here   –
–   *there*   –
passing   through   each   version
like   a   tragic   round.

●

The world is full of murder
and words are usually
the first to go. A life runs
its course then full-stops.
There is nothing as pointed
as bullets used for punctuation
and no betrayal like a word
used for ill gain.
Those whose mouths
are filled with darkness
will spend their breaths
repeating alibis and verdicts.

•••

The Man with the Silver Tongue
released a ladder from
between lithe lips. Rung
by rung a life story appeared
until, after a breathless climb,
his very existence vanished
like a forgotten magic trick
or an out-dated dance.
Only then did we understand
such a bitter, dark hollow –
now seeding in the quiet
of our knowing.

•••

The heaviness of the years
tests our defences and
questions our beliefs
so when pain is stretched
across decades of silence
a slip of the tongue could demolish
entire histories. Consider
those troubled snakes
unlikely to leave their skins
at the foot of an altar. A pounding
in the head breaks
into sad song.

- *(Static, spool)*

Listen:

  there's a hunger in the air. It's reciting prophecies.

    It's doubled up.

Listen:

  the sea roars and wakes throughout the night,

    a troubled sleeper in a land of ephemera.

Listen:

  what was once noiseless and hopeful

    has uncovered alien eyes and left the ghosts chattering.

●

The Dead Man's name is a bruise
          on our tongues.

We reach into our souls to sing.

      We sputter stale air and
      he loses his place in mortal thoughts.

     ...

The Dead Man's voice is the skin
          of a drum

thin from war and constant crush,

      a journey's spine twisted over
      ashen waste.

     ...

The Dead Man's body is holding
          out for judgement.

It turns like a star in a sea of sky

      counting each regret as it is pulled
      further away from its anchor point.

     ...

The Dead Man's luck is a litany
of woes.

In life he marched to a broken beat,

in death the crackle of suspension
fills his tired shoes.

Luck leaves
when unlucky men speak.

• *(Intersect)*

Find a surgeon.
Find a spirit guide.
Find two spare hearts
   to host the vast
   loneliness of death.

Find a monster.
Find a snake.
Find slow days:
   a measure of missing milestones;
   he is all action, no core.

• *(Biopsy)*

He is a man carved from witness wood
and tonight they will cut him open.

Whispers ate his tongue
and people failed to ask after him.

As they tear at his flesh to let in borrowed light
his body splinters and edges its way under their nails.

No men with warmth in their fingers or an inkling
of privacy, no women with a shred of public sympathy.

They fling his body open.
They dismantle him with effortless crime.

Behold the human mess inside   cue a surgeon's wail.
Blood-and-bone strokes warped beyond recognition.

What ages he has lived through   what ruinous tides have
claimed him   not unlike the waters that claimed the SS *Ventnor*.

And having cast off the grain of his years into hallowed seas
he traded fear   for a nightmare of snakes.

Inside he could be dancing
his feet as light as music.   Inside he could be snow.

Extraction after extraction   there is no consensus
on who will keep his soul, who will keep his bones.

When their cruel exercise is over
when they have retrieved   what they never needed

what remains is a man of a thousand regrets.
The insects bury themselves in his swollen dark.

• *(Holding)*

Constantly out of reach,
your heart a hurricane.

How does one die faster?
                you ponder.

To finally arrive at golden fields
or a calm sea   or anything soft, anything welcoming.
Just not this nothingness, this state of restlessness
where crestfallen tides
appreciate your company
but have no regard
for your spiritual well-being.

You wish you had known
this would be disaster, your body pulled
through night after night
trying to hold
on to the earth.

It has done you no good
to bury yourself in silence
and after all   men are nothing
but creatures of survival who
would worship a godly fire   but
if it came to it   would kill it
at any hint of threat.

The shreds of your will
beg for answers – but who or what
do you plead with?
You count in circles.   Hands, feet
in suspension   invisible splinters
edging under your skin.

Faster.

          Faster.

You gasp for air
but it's not air you breathe here,
it is a solemn assembly
of words left unspoken or unheard.

I used to be just like you.

They claimed good will
and mutual understanding
but they only know to keep
their hands to themselves,
such as they are entranced
by the man with the gun and his echoes.

All around them the gathering
of blame and gossip interrupts their thoughts.
A name will be passed around
until it too forgets   it is a name.

If only they knew death   *real death*
the consequences of not being
able to truly let go, a memory slowly erased,
they would find a way to shepherd you to safety.

Look to the west   then to the east.

Steel-eyed eventide
lips   and hands   and feet   and throat
blue from grasping at something

constantly out of reach,
your heart a hurricane.

•

It's a mess.   The fantails tear the dawn apart
with their insistent song and

songs just don't matter much when you're dead,
when it's one evacuation   to the next.

There are bells that ring through every storm
regardless of occasion   leading songs of faith

and redemption   coloured by the strength of hopeful voices.
But now   after Luck's last cards have delivered my fate

the bells do not go easy on me   their mortal peel
forever in my head   sending each regret   spiralling

out of control   crashing through the living
until someone cares to listen.

When life is a bag of snakes
forever looped   in its own disappearing act

with no alibi to speak of
all you can do is wait for them to call for you

          weigh your unlucky heart
and ascend into the gallery of lost names.

• *(Rituals)*

Without light and breath
you fall from here
    but return   led by
        threads of smoke

to find a place set for you at each meal
incense burning by the front door
    and mirrors covered so as not
        to alarm you of your passing state.

The living   strip themselves of red
and leave their hair to grow.
    There are the duties of the living
        to guide your transition –

to prepare ghost money
and joss relics to burn.
Such necessities will secure
  your comfort in the next life –

the clothes, the house, the fortune
of a different man.
But without any of this
  you are left to wander

your empty half-life with no direction.
Until someone wails to mark your absence
until those fires burn everything
  your future reduced to ash.

•

approach—ascend—absorb

the matter is settled

serpentine and shadow lace drawn

down to keep the omens out

the dead man surrenders his voice

but gifts it to his fellow countrymen

allocated—agreed—affirmed

•

Night of nights   enshrouds itself in silence
and deepens the roots,

the terms of your wandering
known only to those who hold you back from closure.

Your craving for finality
leaves no signal –

put your ear to the ground
and wait.

                    (The silence will crush you.)

This life leaves men alone.
The only lesson: death comes to all.

        ...

Now your onus is to surround
yourself in objects   of your former permanence:

a bone flute that stores folk songs and lullabies within,
chopsticks that remember the taste of every meal.

These things won't be burnt and offered when the time comes.
These things have been left to rot in their own deaths.

Funerary custom   astray in a stolen land
reducing you   to man as machine or man as channel.

The Ghost Who Wanders, what do you seek?
You find nothing.

•

History and Memory
meet to divide
the products of Time's fantastic machinery.

On one hand, the dust of wars
and names deemed consequential,
those that died young with still so much to offer,

stories of heroes and moments of national glory.
Everything else is left
for tongues to disremember.

　　　...

A case for murder –
it echoes in two modes:
statistic　　　　or artefact.

Something conspires
in the passing of facts and we are left
with nothing but song.

　　　...

Lionel's legacy in the history books:
racist, murderer.
But where is Joe?

Ah –
　　he's with Lionel.

•

The honeymoon is long over.
There are no chrysanthemums,
no happy anecdotes. Where rats
have festered and gnawed
at the foundations is the smear
of incense ash and old rice.
There is no funeral
waiting for him here, no choir
at the ready asking *Whose name?*
Whose life story? To whom
does our grief belong?
This man alone must face
the reality of death
and the silent drop
into anonymity. No roots,
no branches. Just the dry
song of autumn leaves
collected by the wind.
So they wrap up
his shell and ship him
to Hong Kong, where
out of the way he becomes
a faraway reminder.
Distance will carry
his secrets and take the weight
of his life off their shoulders.
He won't haunt their conscience
or ignite their doubts
with his ghost-hold.

I rest now with my tongue silenced, words
cast out beyond my reach.
The night
embraces all, still as a headstone.

It is a stunning stillness, one that
living,
breathing men
dare not disturb.

If only they had the courage to tear
it down and start anew
to resuscitate
the pinhole sky and imagine once again

a blank canvas destined for greatness.
Instead they cower at the thought of change
and stand by
their fears, softly mouth apologies.

•

How I died in a year of snakes –
    how shame, how murmurs
    still echo in the gauzy frame of night –

    how coiled, how aged
my story slow-drips, best
    left forgotten –

how I cast submission into the weakness
    of joints and watched unspoken hopes
stagger under weight of wrongful death –

    see then those fading steps
    an untethered rhythm left to roam,
a tender lick of the wound –

how their sightlines always bypass me –
    gazing past pain and neglect, they scan
    the scene for victory, a major chord –

how I died with this all unsaid
    and he lived to breathe life into
every single last one of his damned delusions

    making his noise heard
    until they grew wary of his dark
    and committed him to locks –

    how at the final turn
    the snake escaped death
    and later claimed the greatness of the Messiah –

how years, how grace
became but distant souvenirs
of the light –

how my head hums, how my heart folds
at the mere act of acknowledging this
deal with danger –

how my space retrenched
when my eyes gave in
to the longest blink –

then I found myself a thread contained
in time, anonymously familiar –
how I died in a year of snakes.

•

He wore a distinct bravery on his face. Those hands were ready
        for virgin soil or rock; that back was braced for a country
        load. So began a full-heart voyage into the uncharted
        arriving untethered at the deep end of the earth.

Suppose he held a map: the dashed lines to be followed
        may have lead to a golden end, a resolution
        worth his sacrifices. Maybe then his name would ring
        with triumph, not the hushed shame of a broken voice.

Even in his darkest days he sensed how bright the world
        could be, how light might reframe his most dreaded fears.
        Those glints he caught were sure shots: warm on his face
        but sharp on the eyes. He reached out.

He was a moon chasing elusive dawn. He was fire
        in an unlucky year. He was sky torn from the coats
        of giants. He was blood in the roots of ancient trees,
        forever measured by the shadows they leave.

•

Peace is a loose ideal for the abandoned
left to sing their songs
to themselves.

You will never find peace
in your afterlife –
it is the grail so out of reach.

And you will never seek vengeance
because such a lie
could never stir in your heart.

    ...

You wished for water and received
a storm. And with want of sunlight
the stars explode.

    ...

They have shipped your body home
where proper respects will be paid
and offerings made in remembrance.

No longer will you navigate this shift
solo, afraid of the thoughtless tides
the future can bring.

Even if his name still hooks to yours
there will be voices to say your name
to clear the way. The rest is up to you.

Acknowledgements

My thanks to the editors of the following publications, in which some of these poems first appeared: *Essential New Zealand Poems: Facing the Empty Page*, *JAAM*, *Landfall*, *Poetry New Zealand* and *Takahē*.

Thank you to the New Zealand Society of Authors for providing me with a mentorship to assist with the completion of this collection. My most heartfelt thanks to Siobhan Harvey for her enthusiasm, generosity and guidance as a mentor and champion of my work.

I'm also grateful to the many people who provided feedback and encouragement at various stages of this collection's gestation: Bill Manhire, Chris Price, Sam Prescott, Louise Wallace, Andy James, Rajeev Mishra, Renee Liang, Jacob Haronga and my MA classmates.

I have endless thanks for my editor, Anna Hodge, and the team at Auckland University Press. Thank you to Greg Simpson for his spectacular cover design.

I'm fortunate to have the love and support of an incredible circle of friends and family. I raise a glass to you all.

Finally, love and thanks to Dad, Mum and Leight.

Index of titles and first lines

PHOTOGRAPH BY SKLEE

Born and raised in Lower Hutt, Chris Tse is a writer, musician and actor. Tse was one of three poets featured in *AUP New Poets 4* (Auckland University Press, 2011), and his writing has been published in various journals and anthologies in New Zealand and overseas. He lives and works in Wellington. *How to be Dead in a Year of Snakes*, Tse's first full collection, was shortlisted for the Ockham New Zealand Book Awards in 2016.